MW00812762

Mexican Bird

Brown Wings Through White Clouds

MEXICAN BIRD

Brown Wings Through White Clouds

Luis Lopez-Maldonado

QUERENCIA

Querencia Press
Chicago, IL

QUERENCIA PRESS

© Copyright 2024
Luis Lopez-Maldonado

All Rights Reserved

No reproduction, copy or transmission of this publication may be
made without written permission.
No paragraph of this publication may be reproduced, copied, or
transmitted save with the written permission of the author.

Any person who commits any unauthorized act in relation to this
publication may be liable to criminal prosecution and civil claims for
damages.

Cover art: Mia V. Espinoza

ISBN 978 1 959118 82 4

www.querenciapress.com

First Published in 2024

Querencia Press, LLC
Chicago IL

Printed & Bound in the United States of America

Advance Praise

"Luis Lopez-Maldonado's poetry collection, *Mexican Bird*, is a stunning exploration of self, weaving together the personal, political, and social. His poems recall those of fellow queer Chicano poet Francisco X. Alarcón and their penchant for verse rich in cultural nuance and specificity. The musical conduct of these poems are brilliant and memorable, yielding surprise and inevitable suddenness of imagery across carefully crafted lines. They are brave in their encounters with human situations and immigrant voices. They embrace vulnerability juxtaposed with passion. I can say with great confidence that this collection will not disappoint! Truly this is a book worth reading!"

—Ernesto L. Abeytia, series Editor for *The Digging Press Poetry Series*

"Poetry writes itself on our bodies" while "[l]ips are sewn into a new smile." Which is to say: this poemario, in the best of its pieces, compellingly marries language y cuerpo so that "threaded eyebrows [start] / to grow in all directions / like spines on cacti." All throughout the poems in *Mexican Birds*, the portraiture in play, some of it stark, pulls no punches—"[t]he blood stains /No longer stains / But art." And so, says this fierce speaker: "[K]iss open my lips and look inside my mouth, in search of music."

—Francisco Aragón, author of *After Rubén*

I would like to thank everyone who read my poems and offered feedback from day one, from colleagues, to mentors. *Gracias.* To all those magazines and journals that gave most of these poems a home at the start of my career; I am forever grateful for your love and support. This collection of poems is dedicated to my *familia*, though some do not deserve it, and to the few friends I consider family as well. Here is to all of you. Cheers!

CONTENTS

Author's Note

This collection of poems is a melting pot of today, tomorrow, and yesterday; pre-COVID-19. These snapshots were born from my current interest in culture, religion, love, sex, and death.

I am fascinated by the interconnectivity between these universal subjects and the infinite ways they can shape words. Through out these poems we see these specific themes develop and unfurl personal histories. I am addicted to sharing the unshared.

In the midst of change, we must adapt to our surroundings and accept the natural act of transformation, not as bullets to the heart, but as serenades to the sky. With this thought floating above me as I fingered my keyboard on random nights through out the years, I ventured out by exploring loneliness and loss, attacking social issues to create and re-create poetry that represented me—whatever "me" means. I also took the initiative to question everything about me and my surroundings and used popular poetic devices to drive my words crazy, trying to make sense of why our world is so fucked-up at times. I will speak for those that can't, scream for those that are afraid, and fight for those already dead.

I believe there is beauty in between every crack you can find on this earth, even in crack itself. All you have to do is turn your cell phone off and re-connect with the little things in life that really matter. Let yourself love and be loved.

Forward & Onward,

Luis Lopez-Maldonado

MIGRATION: feathers

Brown In White America, *Chicanismo*

I am a *Mejicano*.

Latino

Hispano

Chicano—

or whatever I choose to call myself

these days—because I live in a country

which wiped out all my history,

put an end to my people's ways.

All I have now are the names

discussed in my *Chicano* Studies course

at the University of California Riverside,

names that fought for the brown people and

were chased, caught, and murdered for being

Mexican, for being heroes—

Zapata!

Murrieta!

Hidalgo!

Morenos!

Villa!

Espinosas!

These men once had power,

even gone and dead now, their triumphs

gave color to the *Chicano* Movement,

a time when my people said no more, *basta*!

And raised their voices as one

and chased the ~~American~~ *Chicano* Dream.

I am a *Mejicano*.
Americano
Californiano
Paisano
Estudiado—
An Orange County guy
raised in a white neighborhood
bleeding into whiteness, but I bloomed,
saw that my white "friends" didn't really
like the brown, teachers too, that they
believed Christopher Columbus discovered
this land, was here first, that my people
were only good for cleaning homes
and picking strawberries, oranges.
I am an American.
I am a Mexican.
I am Spanish.
I am *Azteca*.
I come from those before me,
from *tortilla* connoisseurs,
from those that drink *tequila*
to celebrate life's glorious colors.
I come from those that call *Mejico* their
home—the red, white, and green.
From those who pray to *la Virgen de
Guadalupe* in time of need,
in the times when the Texas Rangers shot
them down for being Mexican,
in times when the zoot suit riots broke out
and pinned my people down.

I am a *Mejicano*
who seeks nothing more than equality,
to be seen as a man, not a brown man,
just a man,
to be able to drive sports cars
without being stared at,
to be able to walk into Nordstrom and get
help like all the other white people do.
But my dreams fade away like my mother's
failed education and the defeated people,
the Mexicans, continue to hop the boarder
not knowing that the grass is greener on the
other side, yes, but that it is also
contaminated as well.

Dealing With Being Mexican

Consider this: We are people without history.
My friend Daryll said so
and I believed it.
Night turns to day and I

still wish I was Black though, not Brown.
Mi mama y mi papa used to call me
negrito, I am the tannest in the family.
I don't fit in any family portrait:
Light skins, curly hair, my father's blue eyes.

The dead must wait to be judged,
but here we do that for free to each other,
like how you judge this poem,
like how a White lady's poodle barks

at a colored man. Go ahead and name
your daughters something you never
had. Who knows, maybe one day you can
just call her Heather.

The moon seems to float tonight,
or maybe hang, dead,
like the slave in the corner
hung from a tree
50 years ago—a gay man
hung last week in *Zacatecas, Mexico.*
If not for our color, for our lifestyle…

Because our skin
is not detachable,
we will remain
colored 'til death claims us.
This is a fact, *mi vida.*

I am like the parrots
that fly over boarders,
transcending themselves to another
season, another place,
soaring above the ground
to find their territory claimed by another—
the dove.

Alajuela **In August**

The mist hits my face
My eyes close,
Inhale,
Exhale,
A gentle smile opens them—
Magia Blanca Waterfall—
Thousands of gallons
Crushing to nothing,
To everything,
Green palms
Growing up into the blue,
Tiny orange frogs with yellow eyes
Sticking to everything,
To nothing,
My hands sliding on the wet railing,
Smooth as glass,
My backpack becoming heavy
With moist,
With fear,
Knowing that a jump away
Lies heaven.
I scream into the wind
Thinking I will be heard,
But nothing returns,
But an echo,
The sounds of the songs
Of Costa Rican birds,

The squeaking of my tennis shoes
As I continue down the narrow trail,
Not knowing what is beyond
The white fog,
Not knowing what is beyond
Nothing...

1960...

CALIFORNIA

eyes wide closed,

Mí Abuelito carrying his Mexican dream for a better

tomorrow

like the bright candy inside a piñata, but worse:

he hid inside the trunk.

a pale yellow 1955 Chevrolet...a brave older white woman

suffocating, sweating

he held his hopeful choppy breath

held it, and held it...

the smell of the infinite ocean, seaweed, palm trees galore

he had entered the city of SAN DIEGO.

at last

a fresh start, an opportunity of gold

work, make money and send it to my grandmother in Michoacán

Felicidad!

a tear slowly crept down his pink cheek...

still trapped inside this American product

he opened his eyes

an awakened puppet

Get up at 4am, work all day picking strawberries, then go home and sleep,

the trunk opens...

EL NORTE.

There Are Bodies

Bodies stacked like pancakes,
Strawberry syrup turned blood,
Limbs sticking out like spider legs,
The Mayan sun shining down
Boiling the dead.

Blacks hung from trees,
Mexicans too
We just never hear about it,
Jews burned alive,
The eerie cries of a hundred cats
The glittering stars wrapped around their arms,
Gays decapitated and cut up like a puzzle—
Find me if you can.

These grounds hold truths untold,
Blood dried and covered with rich new soil,
Laws like in Arizona—
Laws banning freedom from freedom—
Dead bodies in history books erased
Put in storage,
To make the white people look whiter
To make America more united.

Immigrants the fuel to this country,

Cheap labor making the rich richer

The poor poorer,

Making it easy to ignore the pool guy without papers

The babysitter without a driver's license

The carwash workers without education

The hotel maids without equal pay—

But you keep hiring them

Humiliating them

Using them,

Thinking that it's wrong

For ~~illegal immigrants~~ undocumented individuals

To come into this country—

Well, except for the Mexicans

That help you with little Emily,

With keeping your house clean,

With sleeping with your husband

When you are gone

~~To see your lover in New York City~~

On work trips—

But you don't hire illegal help,

Oh no,

They have papers

They have papers

I found them through an agency—

In other words,

You found them on the corners of Home Depot,

In the Mexican grocery stores

You like to go and get your *tamales* from,

Like *Cardenas* and *Vallarta* and *Northgate*.

These bodies, dead or alive,
Are brown bodies
Bodies trained to survive
Bodies with Indigenous blood
Running through their veins,
Nameless bodies in search
Of something more than cheap labor,
In search of something more than the American Dream
In search of something more than strawberry syrup
Whipped cream topped with pecans—
Stacked ~~pancakes~~ bodies, heads missing
Their organs stuck inside black plastic bags
Empty tags attached to nothing,
Their souls lost in the dessert
Still trying to get across the boarder
Still trying to find a way out of hell
And into the other side of the fence,
To the land where they serve you
A glass of milk with your pancakes.

Desamparado, Helpless, And Wondering

Esta noche you will listen to me read poetry as you give me head, it will be raining, the bronze chimes will dance around, the palm trees slightly swaying, the pool water will shiver. Where are the butterflies and the bees? You will ask. And I will tell you that I don't write about butterflies and bees a n y m o r e. I will instead flood you with scars of my body, times when I stared at the mirror and thought about the imperfect reflection I caused, the image of an unwanted son. You will listen when I tell you "I fell" and now am sewing myself back together again, stitch by stitch, dead pieces of me under his fingernails, drops of blood like pomegranate juice sprinkled on the sheets; my thirteenth birthday. I am not going to tell you about flowers and birds. *No soy poeta romantico.* I am not a love poet. I don't turn kisses into metaphors about the ocean or make you imagine my life as a beehive, my mother the Queen B. In my poetry I don't like to talk about the "heart" because mine was broken, over and over again. This isn't a happy/dippy/nippy poem either, at no point during this poem will I earn cliché, let me be clear: I did not cry while writing this poem. I sit here, laptop open, hot cocoa spiked with vodka, I type poetry trying to find my own reflection in words I cannot see clearly. I sleep with one eye open, the other one wandering alone in someplace where g r a v i t y does not exist and the sun never disappears.

27

I Love Being Brown But I Don't Love It

I love piping hot *tamales de rajas y frijoles*
The extra *salsa* on the side &
How only Mexicans know how
To really make them, rinsing
The corn husks overnight &
Placing coins at the bottom
Of the pot when cooking them
        But I don't love

I love wearing *el trio de colores*
Red White & Green &
The crocodile boots
The color of red sand &
The bracelets made of string
In the *plazas de Michoacán*
By the tired hands of an
Eighty-year old man
        But I don't love

I love that I love to say
I'm stuck in between
Neither here or there or
Anywhere & not Mexican enough
Or American enough &
Not dark enough &
Not light enough
        But I don't love

I love *Vicente Fernandez* &
Brittany Beyoncé & Gaga
Ketchup with my *torta*
Wine with my *tacos*
Fourth of July &
El Grito de Independencia

But I don't love

HABITAT: bird cage

Death And *Menudo*

I.

I sit here staring at the art before me:
an avocado, too ripe to be displayed
in a blanket of *queso fresco*, topped off with
Tapatio, a plate of chopped onion, another
with fresh *cilantro, oregano,* and salt.
Out my window the skies
are starless.

II.

The black sky threatens the beaten moon,
and I smell my white carnations. There are
more religions on earth than happy souls...

Silence sits with me tonight, with its absent
music, lifeless, drinking black wine.

III.

My hands smell of *menudo con patas.*
I chop dead life, cow tripe, stomach,
cartilage, feet, and sometimes tongues
with a butcher knife and think of murdered
children singing a lullaby. The kitchen reeks
of urine and blended *chile*
as it cooks over night.

IV.

Like sweat, the blood on my hands
drips down. A black dove taps the
glass of my window and I reach
to open it to receive the messages
of the dead. The October breeze
makes me shiver, leaves me
nameless, like a soldier who cannot
talk to Jesus because his mouth
overflows with the tags of the lost.
I have never been able to talk
to Jesus, on this day or any other day.

V.

Some people you think you know all
your life, but I don't even know
myself tonight.

I didn't take the medicine today for
my cholesterol, my low blood pressure,
because I wanted to feel free, no constraints,
no control. I still sit here alone though,
I look at the boiling pot and see the dead
growing old.

On Visiting *El Granjenal, Michoacán* After My Grandfather's Death

Abuelito, the night was black, starless, and the wind brushed the dry *maíz* in the distance. I held grandma's white candle with the image of *la Virgen de Guadalupe* as I walked, illuminating the rocky path to the back of the house. I slowly opened the rusted door to the shack, made of dry cow droppings and hay, all my *abuelito's* labor. The wind yawned and whistled outside, my heart began to pound. I closed my eyes and listened to the music of silence within me.

I imagined black doves outside, hovering over the horse stables, making little flutters of conversation. The pigs would wake up, eat, move places within the *granjas,* and go to sleep again. The rose bushes would bloom, black roses, and then retire as the doves, dark like the night, would pierce them with their long beaks. I imagined walking out of this place and floating through the cornfields, smiling, thinking my soul had been saved too. The chickens would stare and lay golden eggs. The wind, carrying me, would keep me cold all the way to the river, where the black water would shimmer as the beaten moon smiled down at me. My feet would touch the water, sending chills to my chest, and I would cover it with my hands, a memory of being baptized.

I opened my eyes and everything disappeared. Someone was knocking on the door, telling me to hurry up. *Hola mijo* a soft voice said. I opened the door and saw his hair move as his shadow stood in front of me. I stepped out with my eyes closed, holding my candle and reciting a small prayer for the dead. My heart pounded faster, over and over again. The wind blew the flame of my candle out and I walked slower every step I took forward. I opened my eyes to an army of black birds, black doves. They stood still congregating in front of the door.

The floor was covered in scraps of dead rabbits. Beaks shot down to the stained cement for a quick snap of fresh kill. A shadow stood behind me: *Aristeo.* I could feel it floating. I didn't turn back but rather walked through the vultures and into my grandmother's home.

On Life, Drag And Loneliness

People with glassy eyes
stare into the blue
biting their thin fingernails
with nothing better to do,

black bread stacked on the table
a half-empty gallon of milk,
a limp orchid,
and on a chair, some red silk:

that dress was on sale for $49.99.
Curls hang from a hanger hung in the closet
8-inch heels on the floor
and in the room next door,

you fuck some fat bitch
you don't even know.
There is black beneath my fingernails
my palms hard and calloused like the bottom of my feet,

and outside the wind bends dead stones.
Tonight, I can't sleep:
perhaps we die inside our dreams,
too often it seems too real

but I close my eyes and hear the silence,
foreign tapping, the sound of 100 honeybees
and my heart pounds, falls and rises rises and falls
and then,   there is no then,   just an end.

People with glassy eyes
stare into the black now
whispering to the tilting skies
How has life come to this?

Gin And Tonic

I cup my hands to your mouth,
Your hairy armpits exposed,
Your thick legs gripping my back,
Tell you not to moan so loud.

A drop of my sweat falls on your chest,
My bed never felt so good.

I stare into your Italian eyes,
Trimmed eyebrows,
Long eyelashes,
And wonder why you fell in love with me.
You circle my nipples with the tip of your tongue,
Bite me here and there,
Whispering in my ear *Bello*,
Sometimes *Bella*,
Your hips pressing into mine.

I hear a door open, then close.
My grandma is up again,
Her brain and 80-year-old hips
Don't like to rest,
My whole body hurts, she tells me.
In one week she will end up in the hospital
And will die just after Christmas.

I lean in for a kiss,
Your breath stinking of drunk,
But I like it,
Locking lips and hips,
My long black hair falling over your ears,
Your long tongue slipping in my mouth.

A bottle of gin half empty,
Candles burning to nothing,
To everything,
And a blank moment, then silence.

But tonight will never repeat,
The dying slant of September or October
Will come and go
And you will disappear,
Like the ink in this pen,
Tell me we needed time apart,
You needed time to think.

Everything comes to an end:
And now when I think of you,
In the next room,
Everything   collapses.

Just Loneliness

Yes, my grey *guayabera* is on the floor
And I've forgotten what my name is.
My hands cover my face like a bride's veil
As the black smoke slowly disappears,
A *Frida Kahlo* ashtray sits on my lap
Holding dark debris from my Marlboro.

An old notebook sits on my desk
Starring at me like an alarmed black owl,
Frozen with its claws gripping a eucalyptus branch.
A busy, cold night—the last of what's left of summer.
On my desk is a photograph of *el amor*—
A white dress pressed alongside a black suit.

Today, I grow tired of the sounds of the sea.
I sit alone, undressed
Listening to the Oaxacan songbird concerto instead.

Like the sea, I grew annoyed with love,
And also with God, to whom I am just another stranger.
The waves crash, one on top of the other—spindrift rises
Like the soul that once floated inside me.

Mexican Bird

I will die somewhere in New York City
on a cold night,
black flowers will grow from the ground
and the moon will be nailed to the sky
interrupted by fashion ads and LED lights.

In the final hours
I will feel roads inside me
twisting and turning, like knots,
to find only a dead end, no way out.
Moriré
wearing my black leather boots,
a pack of cigarettes on the inside
of my worn sports-coat,
a Las Vegas lighter in my pocket—
one cigarette left,
turned upside-down,
the lucky one.

I want to "people watch" before I ship off
to the next life,
the next chapter,
pay attention to the way they move
their legs,
to the way they tug
on their *camisas*,
to the way they finger
their cell phones
when crossing the street.

Simple things like this to remind me
of how easy life could have been,
of how the human body
is always in constant motion.
It will then be my turn to gasp
for that one last breath,
for one more memory
before it fades forever—
but my heart, dead long ago,
somewhere in *Mexico*.

I need my family to find
my hidden poems about themselves
inside my laptop,
the password unknown to all
but hidden underneath
my Tiffany & Co. porcelain jewelry box.
Words I could not say to them
will be in capital letters,
some in bold and some in italics,
but in a language unintelligible to them—
click, tab, click click—
but nothing will be found,
only a bunch of poems
which they will have no interest in,
they won't even bother looking into them.

Luis Lopez-Maldonado ha muerto.
He will be found with one arm missing
or maybe a leg,
a gold rosary around his neck,
his face half smashed, half open.
His wallet will be missing,
his watch cracked
along with his wrist,
and his invisible wings
will lay limp with holes
hovering over him—
"fly like a bird and fade away."

Dancing With Poetry

I stretch my hands to the sky reaching for something unknown, my brown fingers stretched beyond reality, creating an endless line of energy, the long legs of a ballerina, and my toes go on relevé, my torso suspends like a floating balloon, my ~~chest~~ heart faces up and out. This moment is frozen in time, like a photograph, your eyes glued to mine—we are infinite, you and i. Poetry writes itself on our bodies like tattoos, you the ink across my face and stomach, the rhythm beneath my fingernails, the way the lights only light up half of my body, the other half lost in the darkness, nowhere to be found. i float for what seems like eternity, balancing on two feet, blisters and cuts between my toes, my *corazón* shooting up into the blue as you whisper an i love you, or an i hate you, it doesn't really matter. Words are tattooed on my hands too, your metaphors sneaking up my pink shirt and across my wide back— an infinite field of roses grows inside of me. Lights out. The open door to the dressing room is your breath, cold, mysterious, and longing for someone to step through.

Tallahassee, FL

The grass is always green,
the tombs wet,
the gates constantly open.
I drive by the Old City Cemetery
everyday,
wonder who is buried there,
if they walk at night,
spreading their hands across the sky,
smiling at the little things in life,
or death,
it doesn't really matter.

The crackling light of January
sneaks up on me this morning,
my mind splits in two,
my lips too,
the cold air stings
like a bee.

Orange dahlias never bloom
this time of year,
but at Wal-Mart they do,
so I buy them.

My feet try not to step on the dead,
they say it's bad and disrespectful,
that they will scare you at night,
pull on your feet,
whisper from inside your closet,
smile from underneath your bed.

But unlike these forever young flowers
between my hands,
the grass will eventually stop being watered,
the tombs will dry,
and the gates will rot and crumble like this one:
Mark Conway, Loving Son, 1968-1987,
Rest In Peace Angel.

I cover his name with the orange blossoms,
pretending I know him,
whispering his name into the wind,
rehearsing an Ave Maria for the hell of it,
thinking back to when my grandmother used to tell me
she didn't want a funeral,
no one to shed tears in her name,
no flowers thrown over her casket,
inside her casket—

I smile down at the tomb
knowing my grandmother is
2,239 miles away from me,
buried six feet under
in Orange County, CA:
and in the distance,
a flock of birds,
the sun rising,
the silent screams
of a newborn.

Driving Home From Irvine Valley College

The simple things in life
haunt me tonight. Rain hits
the windshield like bombs
in Afghanistan, & not a single
prayer comes to mind for my cousin
who sleeps with his eyes open
& his favorite blanket
now, a M16A2 Rifle.

Black doves, maybe crows,
stare at me. The cold air scares
the silver moon & stars
& clouds that drift by—pitch black.
Flashes of road signs
is all that is visible to me
tonight. Light spills
from the shadows of the dead
laying in their beds of mud & flowers—
Holy Sepulcher Cemetery.
I speed to pass this fast.

Sad violin music, window open,
& the last of what's left of summer.
My stomach turns, making foreign
sounds for the lack of food—
Empty, I stare at the reflection
in my rearview mirror & I am
still not content. I want to look
like the people in Hopper's paintings—
bellas y eternas.

Everything beyond this street
seems to fade the closer I get to it,
like how courage skips generations.
I come to a dead end & look around
to see if this is just a dream,
or a wrong turn. A thorn
penetrates my lung & I reach
for another cigarette
inside my glove compartment,
& then lighting strikes. More rain.
A glowing sign reads:
City Villa Park—a wrong turn.

Happy Birthday

for my mother

I have searched
for my mother
my whole life
and I find only
black snakes
on the ground—
forgive me *Mama.*
With eyes glued
shut,
I look in church
beyond God
and ask for help.
Her fuchsia lips,
the crimson lips
of a blooming orchid—
Mama's smile alive
like the blossoms
on a winter tree.
I love the unseen
of your hands'
labor,
and the light freckles
sprinkled on your
chest and shoulders
like cinnamon—

isn't it funny,
when you're gone
and dead,
I start listening?
You are like
a moth in the sky
flying high—
what's left of you
is tattooed
on my back—
a pink butterfly.

!Vivá La Frida!

Quisiera darte todo lo que nunca hubieras tenido y ni así sabrias la maravilla que es poder quererte. – Frida Kahlo

Fresh roses adorn your head
Twist in and out of your perfect *trenza*
                    (the *Frida* braid)
Round like a *tortilla*
Ribbons here and there
Red White and Green
Rojo Blanco y Verde
The way your earrings fall south
Your silk *rebozo*
The Gold ring your *Diego* gave you
Ese Panson!
You light a cigarette
And converse with the stars
La Casa Azul
Sitting on an old chair
Diego nowhere to be found,
His shirts reeking of whores
His lies tattooed on your chest
His *mentiras* tattooed on your *pechos*
You bleed like an open wound
And lay frozen, dead with silence.

Frida: You close your eyes
And make weird noises
                    (moans and groans)

Your black eyes pin me down
And I can see flecks of laughter
Inside of them, deep down
As you bite bitter fruit
And stare at the yellow moon
Pregnant with light
Hanging in the air like *mangos*.

Thirty winters and
Thirty springs
Will never be enough
To erase your face
Your masculine eyebrows
Your full lips
Your *faldas largas*
Your aching paintings
Your blind love,
But it might be enough
To say a prayer or two,
                   (to *La Virgen de Guadalupe*)
Look up into the blue
And try making sense of it all,
Nodding at everything the *gringos* say
Their eyes of wax and
Wine and oil.

But time passes by
Everything passes by,
And in the distance
Beyond fried roses and limp trees,
Constellations burn into nothing,
Into everything—
The Blue House
No longer blue
The blood stains
No longer stains,
But art.

Staring

definition: to look fixedly
or vacantly at someone
or something
with one's eyes wide open,

to look & look &
keep looking at someone
or something
with white eyes &
face & privilege,

to mad-dawg profoundly
to the point of exhaustion
to the phase of annoyance
or something like that
with heavy heart &
judgmental glare

to grab your purse &
bring it closer to you
to look around & memorize
or something
incase they are criminals
or want your whiteness

to look down &
keep feeding oppression
keep feeding ignorance
keep feeding racism:

Staring,
S T A R I N G,
Staring.

SPECIES:color

Day Of The Dead: Orange County, California

The wind screams
to be heard today.
It shakes
my windows,
plucks every leaf
off my trees,
mama's roses tortured
and de-petaled,
the sun too scared
to come out.
November has begun
with the Santa Ana winds,
el Dia de los Muertos—
Mexican ghosts float
from *Michoacán* to California—
they rest inside my room.
And inside my home
an altar drowned
with orange and yellow
Marigolds,
plastic rosaries,
white overused candles,
a ten-year-old tequila bottle,
limes, red roses,
white sugar skulls decorated
with pinks and blues
as if the afterlife
was halfway sweet.

Mamá Concha floats in the kitchen
making grandma *chocolate caliente*
and oatmeal for my father
who still lies in bed
sleeping beyond what is today,
a day where he should remember
his own father,
my uncle too.
But the sun now peaks
through distant clouds
and its whispers seem to fade,
the lost Mexican souls
fly away,
float towards another place
where candles burn
and bodies gather
around bright colors,
photographs of their dead
loved ones
and warm tamales
are left behind
for the invisible
to devour.

I See Through Your Tongue, You Liar, Hanging From A Photograph On My Bedroom Walls

The ocean seems to collapse tonight. You exist, but you are not here. All I have now is this universal blueprint on my left ring finger. I sit here alone though, listening to Madonna, watching Black Swan, and I wonder when your short, stubby fingers will slide into me once more. All those nights you came home and smelled of piss and death. The dirty Mexican boots you left by the fireplace. What am I to do with all this now?

We fucked a guy with a toe fetish once—I always did what you wanted to do. But now I am like a lost cat in the gutter. My prey smell an easy game as I walk by: my ripped jeans, fitted t-shirt, curled eyelashes. I like to pretend I am a movie director, hiding behind a black camera, dressing my shame behind a plastic world. Every weekend is another man, another bed. The exhausted wet rubber hanging on the executives I fuck in hotels like the Sheraton or the Double Tree in Hollywood, California. How can I sleep with strangers? Their ripe cocks expand in me, like a blooming pink dahlia. I miss that.

If you could just come here, turn me inside out again. I long for the brown touch of your body against mine, creating new moans under the half moon. I open my window though and see nothing but a black canvas, not even the stars peek out tonight, just the sounds of lonely grasshoppers on the edge of the window frame and the distant cries of the black waves crashing in and out.

Photografias

I. Halloween, 10 years old

I pretended to be *Pancho Villa* who rode alongside *Alejandro Garcia*, my
grandmother's father, a full Spaniard. I had on black boots and an old military outfit
borrowed from one of my uncles. My hair was slicked back with blue hair-gel from
K-mart. My chest pushed forward and out. I held a long breath for the camera to
capture something that I could be proud of, something that looked fearless and
masculine. I held a plastic rifle in my left hand and hung on with my right to my belt
made from fake copper bullets. My *banderillas* crossing over my immature chest, too
light to feel real. My fake mustache kept itching me, bothering me, kept reminding
me what men put up with back then, posing still for a moment caught and developed
on paper, a memory that will be researched later by men like me. Years later I will
write an essay on my great-grandfather who I eventually would find more interesting
than the man he went to war with in 1916.

II. Nephew, November 2011

His hair reminds me of mine when I was his age, of course mine being a bit darker
than his, my skin much more cinnamon. His pale face hid behind balloons—Mickey
Mouse, Elmo, a gold star, a soccer ball, the number 2—which only cost me three
bucks at the Dollar Tree on Main and Chapman that day. I was broke. I couldn't
believe he was turning two. His large eyes, not yet fully developed, his eyelashes long
and pointing down. A tiny smirk, his fingers reaching for the cake in front of him, one
large candle lit in the shape of the number two. One, two, three! Blow! Say cheese…
he couldn't really talk yet but I knew what he might be feeling, something similar to
what I felt when I was young—confusion on why so many faces were smiling and
clapping, why the foreign scent of *carne asada* lingered in the air and why his father
was no where in sight.

III. Wedding, *Guadalajara, Mexico*

The outlines of my family look like deformed mountains. I was sixteen. I was drunk. I
remember this day because of the bride's brother, a tall Mexican with brown hair, a
shadow on his jaw, pierced ears, and eyelashes that belonged to a doll. He was
beautiful. My eyes are not focused in this picture, not like my family's that all point
the same direction, into the black hole of a lens. His smile caught my eye and I looked
to the right, looked at him, into his eyes. The camera flashed. No one knew then, but
then again, a mother always knows. A year ago, she forbid me from telling my father
about myself—being something that wasn't expected or wanted. I ignore her now, not
because I don't love her, but because God doesn't make mistakes.

A Letter To Emily Dickinson

To Emily E.D.—
27 September 2014

Since I read your letters I cannot stop thinking of you, *especially* knowing that you keep writing little poems and sewing them together, hiding them in your old coats and in between walls. Can you write a poem about me? Just please do not write about the brown skin I cannot strip, about my alcoholic uncle who killed himself last year during Christmas, or about how I sleep with random men when I feel lonely. I would appreciate that. I'm tired of people painting the same image of me.

Dani is here now, came from Texas last week and wanted a place to stay. I know you tell me to stop falling for my ex-lovers, but he is just so damn cute, those dimples and green eyes get me every time!

Like you, I too like to write letters in pencil, smell the lead against thick paper, write poems in ink and use excessive dashes—marks meaning something, or nothing, giving space to words too beautiful to connect. You write of death like it's alive and so do I. I can't stop myself sometimes—poems of black birds, black rivers, black shawls—I kill myself often in my poems.

I think a lot about you, how you are an introvert, a shy and lonely girl; I am an extrovert, always seeking attention and love. But does love really exist? If it does, I have yet to see it and feel it. Maybe I have bad luck. Any thoughts?

How did you manage to write 1, 800 poems? I think about that a lot and it seems like an impossible task. I don't even have time for a glass of wine nowadays, let alone to sit my ass down and write poetry all day. I hate it. I wish I could write that much.

I wonder what you do all day in heaven—if you sit around and write prose poetry, blow them into the blue and let them float away, or if you fly from city to city, whispering in our ears when we get writer's block. What do you do? I will write again. I hope you are well and full of violets and daisies.

Luis.

On Being High And Drunk: #Wheredowegofromhere

I.

~~Conservative politicians dine at the Ritz-Carlton in Orange County, CA and twenty miles away families eat left over beef stew in Santa Ana made from ingredients picked up at the 99 cents store.~~ The Mexican cook at the 5-star *Raya* refuses to take home the end of dinner "extra food," so they end up throwing away $300 every night; the restaurant makes about $100 per table so it's no big deal. Throw that shit out! Juan goes home to his wife's beef stew, having the leftovers, of the leftovers, from feeding three little boys and one girl, kisses Sandra on her forehead and whispers: *Gracias Amor*,

now that   is what fine dining tastes like.

II.

Crickets grind their legs waiting for the sunset to explode and I sip on Syrah or Merlot, at this point I don't really know. Fall is here. I look up at the sky and see headless, handless bodies dancing in the clouds, they look like they have somewhere to go:

delight

has to be   somewhere.

III.

Mrs. Merchon drew testicles and vaginas on the greenboards and we learned how vaginas bleed, about abortion, about masturbation, and saw images of naked people, strangers, front and back; giggles bubbling underneath our lips. When I was in sixth grade I put pins and chalk in his coffee, some laughs, and I topped it off with spit, more laughs. The principal lines us up, bodies facing each other like stars: *Who did this?* I thought I had friends.   I did not.

IV.

I come from hills rolling with oranges, white roses spread like confetti, two-story
homes facing two-story homes, four-car garage doors, iron staircases, marble floors,
heated pools, Botox filled cheekbones: people spending too much $$$
at trending health stores, texting, Tweeting, Tindering.   I come from the
men riding next to *Pancho Villa*, from burnt *tortillas* and cow tongue stew,
from *Michoacán Mexico* and the migrating Monarchs drowning oyamel fir trees
in the winter to escape death and freezing temperatures: frozen oranges, limp roses
and heated pools.

V.

His hips slid between my sheets, black coffee on the side table, black arms and legs,
white smile, white eyes, his beard more like peach fuzz. The moon is pinned to the
sky tonight as we make music between walls, call each other bae and boo,
hoping for an *I love you* but who the hell has time for that:
we end up fucking twice, black skies, black walls, black and brown cocks,
our breath rising

                   from everywhere   like dust.

Sunday Catholic School

He was reading the bible and eating a Milky Way, every bite he took I blushed. His lips a slight delicate pink. Inside me butterflies appeared and disappeared, an imagined prism, a blossoming blue flower expanding, drizzling out from my pores. His hands were smooth, his fingers a bit forceful, his smile reassuring me everything was going to be okay. He gave me something to drink just before, holy water? And it tasted like candy, so I took it. Then in bed, anal love. The dead of winter outside the window, the birds crying out to be heard, the grasshoppers snapping like the striking of a hundred matches. My thing hanging over his face, his tongue swirling around my sack. moans coming from somewhere unknown. Ten years have passed and his smile is tattooed in my memory, his black eyes, the way his gold rosary tickled my neck, his sweat dripping from his hairy chest, *la Virgen de Guadalupe* stitched on his robe. That night I became a man with God. *Ahora ya eres todo un Hombrecito en los ojos de Dios.* I have many more poems to write after this one, poems about hidden bibles in my room, stories about hot priests that pray themselves to orgasms—metaphors mean nothing to a numb body, sentences reminding a boy of the real gift of God.

How i Imagine *Satanas (the devil)*

Your voice sings through the ears of infected hummingbirds fluttering from flower to flower, diseases spreading like butter over toast. You try holding me in your arms as I dance barefoot, leaping in the air and landing in first position. Your six-inch-long nails, sharp like *cuchillos*, caress my neck and glide down to my chest, circling my nipples like vultures, *pajaros feos y negros*. You wear an insectile dress dragging the voices of the dammed like a dead carcass. You open six doors with the blink of your deformed eye—door one offers honey, the next money, door three has flowers, and four power, the fifth gives us laughter and the last conjures a happily ever after. You whisper in our ears to choose one or even two, red lips, your venomous tongue sliding out, split in half, like the tip of a faint-banded sea snake, the most dangerous snake in the world. Your glittering wings wrap ignorant souls that fly above the grounds, not quite into heaven, but close enough for you. At night you hide in fear of my chanting, I pray to God and his son Jesus, *resando tambien a la Virgen de Guadalupe,* asking for protection from them and not from you—your broken halo growing mold, and a photograph, your baby face, an angelic image frozen where space was invisible and age was non-existent.

El Granjenal, Michoacán, December Traditions

I hear a little girl talk to me
on nights like this one, intimidating
and forgotten. When limp
olive trees cast their shadows
on my shadow, *machete* in hand,
I stop to watch. Is it sin to closely
watch your cousin strip down to his underwear?
Uno de los Maldonado's baby cries
and my *abuelita* calls for her *yerba de Manzanilla.*

Las posadas are held tonight on our street,
my sister chosen to be *La Virgen Maria,*
my cousin as *Jose*—horses, a donkey,
floors drowned
in hay, a floating star lit
hung with the same wire
they used to hang my birthday *piñatas* with—
I am no one tonight though.
No role playing.

The warm smell of *canela* boiling in large pots,
pan dulce arranged neatly in plastic
containers. This feels foreign to me,
like my mother and my father.
But I pretend to enjoy it and stand behind the old ladies
in their black *rebosos.* We sing in Spanish,
songs that relate to the Nativity scene
that once was before my time. The space between
my temples fixes on my cousin's eyes
and we both smile under our closed lips.

A choreographed night and after duties disappear,
so do we, sneaking away, taking an extra *aginaldo*.
Going to our private hideout—the muddy stalls
of an abandoned home where a family
was murdered. In the dark we forget
about everything and caress each others hair,
and kiss each other's lips, for practice,
pretending to be doing it to a girl.
But for me, it was
heaven.

Luis Lopez-Maldonado

UV lights reflect on your eyes
Raybans like jailcells
A smile hidden somewhere
Behind the color brown,

Stars hang from earlobes
Turquoise pierces your nose
Like Jesus nailed to the cross,

Your chapped lips hide behind
A Mexican goatee and mustache
Your threaded eyebrows starting
To grow in in all directions
Like spines on cacti,

Why the cut glass around
Your neck? Do you want
Your reflection to slice your throat
Like the soldiers in Afghanistan?
You say nothing only stare
Into the nothingness
As your brown hair
With chunks of honey
Falls on your sore shoulders,

The color pink bursting
On your chest like bombs.

Write A Poem About BROWN Without Using The Word Brown Or I

When God made the world
He thought about the year 2016
He thought about Hitler Part II
#TrumpNation
He thought about the freezing winters
South Bend, Indiana would have,
He thought about how my godmother would die
from cancer at 52
He thought about me:
the color of mud and cinnamon
the color of mocha lattes and cardboard boxes
the color of hardwood floors and over-ripe bananas
the color of cow shit and dust,

When God made the world
There was no Crayola
There was no choice
There was no label
There was no color-coding,

Fuck it:
Brown is brown is brown is brown…

Write A Poem About TATTOO Without Using The Word Tattoo Or I

Piñatas were evil before our time
in times when they were hung
like humans in celebration
to the Aztec God *Huitzilopochtli,*

stressed leather against bronze skin
gold and turquoise drowning
arms and legs and head,

secrets marked on faces
lines intersecting chiseled
jaw and bone, circles stamped
around nipples and bellybutton,

my people pushing heads
down pyramids
one thousand steps
going up toward heaven
toward the sun,

my patria hidden below
angel wings against
brown back,
hidden between heart
and ribs and blood:

growth death decay birth
the scripture of life
scratched into flesh,
the pain no where to be found
only the smell of fresh ink
and burning skin
only the smell of fresh ink
and burning skin.

Write A Poem About SKIN Without Using The Word Skin or I

Bones are hungry children
waiting for Christmas to arrive
       they grind snap crack & pop
Muscles are white ballerinas
smoking during intermission
       they laugh puff puff & stretch
Veins are venomous snakes
curling in & out up & down
       they glide slide hiss & hiss
Skin is mountains hiding
earthquakes before snowfall
       It shakes shivers burns & turns

SURVIVAL:beak

Battle Of *Puebla*, 1862

Margaritas cover black, round tables drowned in chips and salsa, rims outlined in salt crystals, clear plastic straws sticking up into the sky. *Mariachi* guitars and gold trumpets blowing into the ears of bodies dressed in sweaty work clothes—*El Mariachi Loco Quiere Bailar!* $10. *Cielito Lindo!* $10. Today packs every El Torito and Acapulco restaurants here in the OC, $8 valet drivers running to get the white lady's Mercedes as she stumbles with her Louis Vuitton, iPhone in her left hand, her breath stinking of fun, her stress left at the bar during happy hour—Cinco de Mayo! Because this Mexican holiday has turned into an excuse to drink margaritas and Coronas, it's been mechanized and Americanized, and its history has been forgotten, the blood shed in *Puebla* never happened, hundreds of dead men on the muddy floors fought for nothing, fought for white people to celebrate this day with bright colors and *tacos*—the victory of *Mexico* over the French lingers somewhere between the pages of old history books, abused and forgotten. Because Cinco De Mayo is easier to say than *El Dia De La Batalla De Puebla* and because it doesn't matter who won just as long as the margaritas keep coming...

Girl At LAX International Airport

Hundreds of faces
waiting on a number
and the only thing
I cared for was your hoops, Chanel Couture,
black and round, hanging
against your pale face.

You opened your mouth,
and like a song
the Spanish alphabet
widened my eyes. Those fuchsia lips,
painted nails, mascara covered
eyelashes, but you belonged to China,
and you spoke my tongue?

Like a pink butterfly
your lips moved as you spoke
to a beautiful white man next to me.
Your hair fell on your
shoulders, like how the leaves hang
on the branches of a willow tree.

Your eyes locked onto mine,
like when someone catches you
staring at them,
and I turned away to my left. I rarely
blush, but I was afraid you would see
my brown skin turn crimson.
I glanced back, looking to find
your complexion again.

I see you, Asian girl.
Petite, milk skin, curves
in the right places, your delicate
ankles.

Soon though, an empty seat, you disappear,
and another suitcase approaches
to claim that spot—flight 877
departs and I go back to reading
some Christopher Abani poetry.

Starbucks Venti cinnamon dolce latte,
cup on floor, salted pistachios
in my hand, my ticket to Oahu
tucked in my shirt pocket. I turn the page
and I look out and away from the people that stare
at my black nail polish, my hair,
and flowered shoes. Self-conscious, I cross my right leg
over my left and whisper to myself in Spanish:
I am beautiful too.

#HandsUpDontShoot

I think of 2014, and how Blacks are still being killed for being black, #MikeBrown. How the brownpeople are still labeled *illegal*, even when it was the whites who came into our land and killed our people and named it AMERICA. I think of who I am, whom I know, whom I represent: I am the rainbow during the fucking rain. I am the hungry little boy out in the streets. I am the whore in Paris, who lets you penetrate me for $200, cum inside of me for an extra $25. I am the cloth covered Muslim on his knees, praying for who knows what, everyday at the same time, just as the sun begins to set. I am that pretty young Asian girl going under the knife, to look more white—*cut my eyelids off and give me big eyes,* she says. I hide between walls, talk to trapped spirits, steal an ice cream Snickers bar from Wal-Mart, give a fake homeless man five bucks on the side of the road to feed his addictions. We all have addictions. It feels like 1960; cops beating down unarmed citizens, men in heels getting bashed and lost, our President being called a homosexual and a monkey.

#Whatthefuck #Historyrepeatsitself #Godiswatching

Las Manos Del Papa

for Alma

He went in from behind
tearing her insides,
numb face
drowning into a pillow.
Blind.
He reeked of Silver Patron
and his Aztec-chiseled
face
let out curses
in three different languages.
Blood stained sheets,
cum landed
on the floors
like poison
to the earth,
blood-stained sheets.

Pink and white
Barbie underwear
bundled in the corner
of her room,
her body a dead daisy,
frozen in a silent scream
for help.
Sweat on hairy hands and thighs,
his manhood
wet and dripping.
Naked toes trembled.

Dark curls
covered her pale stare
up to the popcorn ceiling.

Thirty years later,
an echo chased by a shadow—
she hides behind
a fake smile:
I can pray no more.
Sad violin music,
Jack'n'Coke
and the pinking horizon
helps her navigate
the nightmares at night.

She sits in a park
writing these memories down
in a poem
and stares
at vibrant little girls
swinging in the air,
flowered dresses,
pink ribbons—
a warm sensation
somewhere underneath.

Surviving In Santa Ana

for Maria Concepción

Just the other day I saw a small Mexican girl, boogers
crusted on her nose and upper lip, sneak into a *panaderia* &
steal a *pan dulce*, the one with the smiley face done
in strawberry jam. Her fingers were sprinkled with sugar
& her eyes floated around to see if anyone had noticed.
The cashiers were busy, the plastic cases filled with bread,
the bakers in the back with their white hair nets punching
the raw dough, molding it. She stepped out of the bakery
following a woman carrying a Mickey Mouse birthday cake
& I followed her. She led me around the corner of the
street into a small neighborhood. I heard her say "*Eh!*
Salgan chamacos." Three smaller Mexican children, two
boys & one girl, came out of a wrecked playhouse
& surrounded the girl. Her hand extended the warm bread
& the kids ripped the bread into three pieces. The girl saw
me approach them & she stood in front of the children,
protecting them. "Sorry, sorry" she said over & over.
Then silence. I reached into my pocket & handed her a
dollar bill, all I had left. Then silence. I walked away before
they saw me cry. As I entered the crosswalk, the little girl
pulled on my shirt. I turned around & she put her dirty Barbie
in my hand.

UCSB, 141 Page Manifesto

for those students that left us too soon

Bullets flew like birds,

the songs of 100 cats crying,

the sweat sliding off his cheeks,

biting down on his teeth,

but sirens around the corner

did not stop him:

three students dead in his dorm,

stabbed to death for being smart,

for knowing the square root of some big number;

The Day Of Retribution.

Shots

       Fired

I don't know why you girls aren't attracted to me

Shots Fired

       6 dead, 7 including Elliot

Humanity, all of my suffering on this world

has been at the hands of humanity, particularly women

       Fired

       Shots Fired.

His therapist called too late,

saw his YouTube video

fifteen minutes too late,

no one noticed

no one cared:

pink lips,

eyes already dead,

driving, speeding,

pulling the trigger
Bang Bang   Bang!
13 injured, punctured lungs and legs
compassion somewhere hidden
between the grass and the sky,
the pinking horizon slowly turning black.

I became more and more depressed
my sex drive was at its peak,
stuck in the void of helplessness
anger   disappointment   virgin
I had nothing going for me in my life:
When they are writhing in pain
their bodies broken and dying
after I splatter them,
they will fully realize their crimes.
I want to kill both UCSB and SBCC students.

The empty street floods with flowers,
and candles
and dry throats,
the echo of 100 silent screaming students,
news stations galore,
the yellow CAUTION tape blocking blood,
blood painting the ground like freckles:
Women are like a plague,
they don't deserve to have any rights;
I didn't start this war,
But   I
                    Will   Finish
It.

At Your Funeral

Something inside my skull pounds, beating like my heart, but worse, the temples by my eyes thumping like a drum. As I fix the crosses and hearts around you, made from red roses, white carnations, and baby's breath, I move the crystal rosary threaded between your bruised and wrinkled hands. Your fingers cold, thinner than before, fingernails painted in a pale passion pink, the same color that you wanted on the day you had your hips replaced. My hands touch your frozen face and I am numb to the way they made you pretty again, your combed hair, your eyelashes covered in a light coat of mascara, your lips glistening with a bit of lip gloss, your cheeks filled with who knows what, maybe cotton or newspaper, but not flesh. You told me not to cry for you when you died but as I fix your collar and your diamond broach, I begin talking to you, *"aye mi viejita, mira que bonita te pusieron"* and my lower lip trembles, reminding me of when I was a kid and how you would defend me when my dad hit me with his belt. But like you, my mother will also end up sleeping in a copper coffin, drowned in flowers, a forced smile shaped by the hands of the make-up team at the mortuary home. I swallow and then cough in your casket, waiting for you to tell me to cover my mouth, but I wait and hear nothing from you, your smile still frozen, your hands still folded below your belly, you sleep in the same position as ten minutes before. I turn my back to you and walk away thinking about the meaning of life—ust one die to live? And like the beating of a drum, or a hundred drums, my heart does not thump any softer as time passes, it gets louder, and louder, one hit after another.

Madre

You smile like the Mona Lisa
thinking I don't notice,
but I do,
your prosthetic teeth
behind your cracked lips
hardly ever get some light,
when you laugh
you cover your mouth with your hand,
embarrassed,
thinking we will notice
that the teeth you chew with
are not yours,
but those from a laboratory.
You caught a gum disease
when you were fifteen
and had all your teeth
removed in Mexico,
plucked like chicken feathers,
and you tried to take your life,
your teeth-less life,
but you failed.
You tell me to brush my teeth,
get mad at me when I come home
from the dentist
and show you that I have six cavities,
and you cry,
tell me again about your teeth,
how you wish you had mine,

how you wish you could explode
in smiles bigger than just a smirk,
explode into laughter like Christmas,
explode away from your scared chuckle—
you point at the fake Mona Lisa
that hangs in my room
and tell me how you think she is beautiful,
how you wonder if that woman in the painting
had teeth like you
or had teeth like me.
You smile.

Texting My Ex On Valentine's Day

I want a bullet to eat my brain,
to shatter memories
from 2003 thru ~~2010,~~ 2011
for it to un-dig my way
thru the tired cliché
of "gay" life.

I am not by any means a Saint
but I pray that my God
hears my ~~lies~~ cries
and helps me
as I numb myself—
flashes of when I knew you,
poems about small dicks,
men too weak to make me feel like a man,
summer nights
driving down PCH
with my windows down,
the sunset too orange
to disappear,
my mouth moving
reciting my name into the wind
that flew by.

This cold metal in my hands
reminds me of you,
knocking holes
in my *piñata*
hoping for something sweet
in the middle,
but I was already
empty—
the loneliness of an echo,
the cry of blind-violence,
the way you will dry
and fall to dust.

This ~~trigger~~ switch
behind my index finger
feels warm though,
like the subtle heat
my grandma's *tortillas* conjured
on Sunday mornings
when my *abuelito Mauricio*
cooked *menudo*
and called everyone to go over—

Why do you all of a sudden
love me now?
Is it because someone
thought you already sat on rainbows
at the age of 8
and took you into adulthood?

Are you afraid of dark water,
of all Saint's Day,
or of the big-black-bird
that sits outside your window
on dry nights like tonight?
Do you wish you could be a stranger
who wastes their life
behind flickering television screens
and prays to the *Virgen del Perpetuo Socorro*?

I text you
question after question
and wait, but no answer,
but as I try to un-dig the past
I only dig myself deeper,
blood flooding my cheeks
as I finger a cell phone
with my right hand,
more questions—
(New Message)
it was not you,
it was me.

Making You Pretty Again

for Marisol

Organs are moved,
Lips are sewn into a new smile,
Veins drained of DNA,
And underneath your bruised chest,
An empty space
Where your heart once was.
~~Thirteen~~ fourteen stitches
In and out of skin,
Blood dripping
From your inner thighs
Like strawberry syrup.

Your milk skin was torn by teeth
Of ~~six~~ men:
One there,
~~Two~~ here,
Another there
And the rest warm in your hands,
In your mouth,
In front of you with a camera.
Your little black dress
Ripped to shreds,
Your blue Jimmy Choo's
No where to be found,
A blue pill in your martini,
And the rest
You said,
You don't remember.

But with this poem
I plant seeds
That will flourish
Into something else
Than what's in front of me,
Maybe an apple tree or cherry tree.

Today:
Your sad eyes,
Your yellow eyes,
Your left too weak to see out of,
Your shampooed hair,
Your dark curls,
And your trembling legs
Not spread-open
Like chopsticks anymore,
But closed,
Crossed,
The way you were
Inside
Your mother's belly
Before you were born;
Untouched
Slouched
Whole.

Being Gay

If I were straight, and my eyes blue,
Then I could have had a life with you.
It would be glorious like the wings of angels.

Yesterday I prayed three Hail Mary's
So that I wouldn't go to hell, and more.
I woke with a beaten expression:
A dream of getting beat for wearing pink.

My brown skin is tattooed on me though,
In me,
And the laughing dead know it.

You littered my path
With your blond curls,
Your long legs. And the eucalyptus
Leaves were crushed by the bottom
Of your bare feet, over and over again.

What of me now?
Like a hummingbird fluttering
Through the blue, I found you.
I sit here all alone, rocking back and fourth,
Imagining what could have been,
And of what it really is; unmatched us.

But I am gay, and my eyes brown,
The idea of you and me drowns.
I am a man that loves other men,
So I will continue waiting for them:
The needing and needing and needing.

Estrella

I stare at myself in the mirror. My eyes are empty with disappointment. All I've had to eat is a microwaved burrito from Ralphs, or Vons, wherever it was I stopped and got my red lipstick. My first time on stage today as the woman I have always wanted to be. My curly hair hanging on the edge of the chair, resting from being inside a plastic bag for who knows how long, waiting to touch my glittered shoulder or cover one of my fake eyelashes. I want my family to be here when I perform Beyoncé's "Listen" but that is only another dream tucked inside of me—the perfect illusion for the dress I am wearing tonight. I touch my delicate cheeks and add more blush, using the brush around and around my freshly shaved face. It's all gone now, my past—the masculine in me. I stand up on my 8 inch heels and blow a kiss into the reflection of beauty. I now walk as a she, as Estrella. Unaware students laugh, or gossip because they are uncomfortable as I glide beside them, the beading on my train making a slight shimmy-shimmy shake-shake sound. Poetry hangs on her mind from the night before and dance boils beneath her tight black bra. Eager faces stare, seats fill, tickets bought to see men dress as women. With one hand holding the bottom of her ruffled dress, she steps up onto the stage, step by step, not alive, not dead, but lost and willing.

Untitled 7

I kneel down and trace my name in the sand with my index finger. There is nothing left in my heart except a few one-night-stands, my brother calling me faggot, my cousin Marilu swallowing pills to kill her baby—someone is waiting for me though, waiting for me to die, to break my bones and drain my veins. They will kiss open my lips and look inside my mouth, in search of music.

Something Missing

for my Father

White vans with black windows,
wheels sparkling
like the clear waters of *Cancun,*
little boys skipping
through pink & blue skies
with purple kites in their hands
their faces w/ crumbs
from an ice-cream sandwich.
But the birds fell
from the branches of the apple trees
frozen stiff
heart-broken
& his world was turned
inside-out, upside-down.

His hands don't lie
on days like this
or any other day,
they're all the same to him
now.
Hands & feet
used as guides,
beat by beat
they touch the unseen,
his ears picking up the steps
ants make the squeak
of the door when someone comes home late,
the silent cries
his wife re-visits every night in the shower.

All he sees is black:
Red roses = black
White snow = black
Blue waves = black
Tan bodies lying on beach = black.

& like those frozen birds
he too became numb
to the pain.
In the mail a blue card
w/ a white stick figure in a wheelchair
a social security check every month
visits to the doctors
when his cholesterol is too high
his diabetes getting worse
his arthritis taking over.
He sits in the cold garage
by himself now-a-days
television turned to a Mexican news channel
raw almonds on white napkin
a game of Texas Hold'em
& in front of him two hands,
one for him & the other he says
"*para mi papa*"

I AM CECIL!

> for all the colored boys that are into boys

Huizache flowers drown the ground
The whiteness of the walls bleeds
Into my body, waist deep in *poesia*,
My brown voice screams inside
A bottle of *1800 Tequila*.

I sip on vintage black wine
And stare at graffiti scarred windows—
Joto! Get out of my town—
And the day never ends, never stops
Counting itself, never notices
Poetry as homophobia.

Humid Spanish moss hangs
Against blueberry skin,
And you speak to me
In the languages of crickets,
Blow a cold breeze my way:
White stars bend down
And I light a Camel Crush.

The birds mock us tonight
Singing in vowels unintelligible
To us: fuck inclusion!
I want to scream and weep and roar
as if we were already dead—
In the distance of an awkward corner,
Orchids dissolve, as if made of sugar.

Balada Para Mi Muerte

Seasons erase your face now
Memories of when we were young
Appear on the dead walls of this apartment,
Smiles frozen in time | snapshots
Times when nothing mattered | but us
Our bodies locking
Blooming flowers—
Homosexuality the noble disease of the artist,

Your blood-shot eyes stare off into the blue
Breath stinking of Vodka & cranberry juice,
You mistake the flies floating above the trash
For stars
& tell me you love me—
The way you said it made me feel | nothing,

I clap my hands in dead silence
Wait for your green eyes to look my way
& gesture with your mouth | invisible words
Floating poetry—
A face turned a patchy red
A mess of black cookies with white filling
A lost bird singing outside the window,

But now there is nothing left of love
Nothing to smile about
No birds outside my window
No color on this pale face
Only a blank page
My arthritis numbing my hands,

The corners of the room starting to mold
Nothing worth writing about—
My little niece asked me what death was like
& I told her it was like going home,
I want to go home.

But you are gone now
Your name still tattooed on my shoulder
Still visible
Moves when I shower,
Hides under the sheets at night,

I told you to burn me when I died,
Where are you?
I am afraid of the dark
& won't be thrown down into the ground
For my bones to rot
To evaporate
& remain trapped in a coffin.
Where are you?

I sit here now, hair like snow,
Wrinkles flooding my eyes & mouth & hands
Waiting for the phone to ring
For the door to be knocked on
For any sign of life—
I light & re-light a cigarette
& begin to see your face
Once more
On the cracked walls
Of my apartment.

Printed in the USA
CPSIA information can be obtained
at www.ICGtesting.com
CBHW070011260424
7569CB00011B/142

9 781959 118824